TIME EXPOSURE

First published in Great Britain 1991
by the Peak Park Joint Planning Board

© Peak Park Joint Planning Board 1991

Set in Goudy WTC by
Altered Images, Nottingham

Printed in duo-tone by
Balding and Mansell, Wisbech

ISBN 0-907543-48-0

*Cover: The population of Derwent
village, 1912, evacuated to make way
for the Ladybower Reservoir (inset)*

TIME EXPOSURE

the Peak National Park ~ Past and Present

Conceived and produced by
Ray Manley

Text by Roland Smith
Design by Karen Sayer and Diane Tranter

Facing page: Crinoid fossils in a gatepost. Millions of sea creatures like these go to make up the limestone of the White Peak.

A Changing Landscape

The landscape of the Peak, just like anywhere else in Britain, is dynamic and constantly changing. It has never stood still, not even during the last 40 years when 542 square miles of the area has been protected as Britain's first National Park.

In many respects, the Peak was a National Park where it was most needed. Surrounded by the sprawling industrial cities of northern England and the Midlands, it was the last unspoilt outpost of the southern Pennines, and a precious weekend escape for the teeming populations created in the wake of the Industrial Revolution. Half the population of England lived within 60 miles of the Peak and, as Prof. C.E.M. Joad wrote in 1946: "In our day, hiking has replaced beer as the shortest cut out of Manchester."

But in his day, many of the highest and wildest moors of the Peak were closed to ramblers. A strictly-enforced exclusion policy was adopted by the owners of the grouse moors so that in 1934, only 12 footpaths crossed 215 square miles of Peak moorland, with none at all over the highest points of Kinder Scout and Bleaklow.

Inevitably, pressure for access to these moors built up, culminating in the famous mass trespasses of the 1930s. Five ramblers were jailed for incidents arising from the celebrated mass trespass on Kinder Scout on April 24th, 1932. As walking became more popular and leisure time increased, it was obviously a situation which had to change.

But access was not the only problem in the Peak. Creeping suburbanisation was spreading unchecked, its mock-Tudor tentacles from the neighbouring cities of Sheffield and Manchester. Incongruous red-brick, 'half-timbered' villas were springing up on many of the main roads which led out into the Peak, and ugly advertising hoardings shouted from many roadside verges. One on the remote Cat and Fiddle road outside Buxton even advertised the attractions of Blackpool, 73 miles away!

Even uglier were the vast limestone quarries belching smoke and dust from the enormous holes they were blasting out of the White Peak landscape. The problem was that this was where the valuable rock came close to the surface, in a place that was easily accessible by road and rail. Rubbish tips appeared on the edge of pretty Peakland villages, where a spider's web of overhead power and telegraph lines destroyed the impression of rural peace. New and ever-busier roads made the Peak even easier to get to, and the fast-growing cities which needed vast quantities of clean water for drinking and industry usually obtained it by the construction of reservoirs which flooded lovely Peakland dales and destroyed their ancient communities.

Among the more horrific incursions that were proposed but successfully fought off by the growing band of preservationists was one for a giant steel works in the beautiful Edale Valley, a proposal hard to imagine today. But bodies like the Sheffield and Peak branch of the Council for the Preservation (now Protection) of Rural England, the National Trust and the Joint Committee for the Peak District National Park were campaigning hard, and the Peak National Park was finally set up under the provisions of the 1949 National Parks and Access to the Countryside Act on April 17th, 1951.

This book attempts to catalogue the landscape changes in the Peak through 'before and after' photographs from the National Park authority's collection, and new ones specially taken by Ray Manley, the Park's staff photographer. In many cases, the photographs show a totally different landscape, almost unrecognisable from today's scene. The reasons for these startling changes are interpreted in the accompanying captions and text, or in Ray's photographic notes at the end of the book.

Most of the earlier, turn-of-the-century photographs obviously predate the designation of the National Park, but others show the changes – both good and bad – which have taken place in the last four decades, the period of the National Park's influence.

The pressures on the Peak have not diminished since the Park's inception. If anything they are growing day by day, making the work of the Park authority increasingly important if we are to pass on an untarnished heritage to future generations.

The book is published to mark the Park's 40th anniversary and shows, if proof were needed, that landscapes can never be fossilised or frozen in time. The Park has always been a dynamic, working landscape and always will be, so long as the people who created it continue to live and work here.

The challenge for the Park authority, and for its residents, is to guide the changes so that the quality of the Park as a place to live, to work or to visit is enhanced rather than diminished.

"Was you ever in Dovedale?"

Members of a cyclists' touring club at the Stepping Stones in Dovedale at the turn of the century.

Dovedale today from the same viewpoint. Latest surveys show that over two million people visit the Peak's most famous dale annually.

A View of the Straits *in* DOVE DALE*, near* Ashbourn *in* DERBY-SHIRE.

Printed for Rob! Sayer. Map & Printseller. at N° 53 in Fleet Street London.

*The romantic, 18th century view of Dovedale,
as seen in an engraving from an early guide
book.*

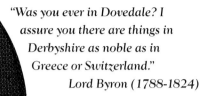

"Was you ever in Dovedale? I assure you there are things in Derbyshire as noble as in Greece or Switzerland."
Lord Byron (1788-1824)

Byron's enthusiastic eulogy to his friend, the Irish poet Tom Moore (who was later to move to Ashbourne) was a typical reaction to the 'discovery' of picturesque scenery by the Romantic Movement in the early 19th century. It was echoed in the paintings of Joseph Wright of Derby (1734-1797) who romanticised Dovedale in a series of water colours, and in Chantrey's delicate engravings.

But the first to publicise the Peak's best-known dale were the angling partners Izaak Walton and Charles Cotton, joint authors of 'The Compleat Angler', first published in 1653. Cotton, who lived at Beresford Hall at the northern end of the dale, lavished fulsome praise on the crystal-clear trout stream.

With the building of the Midland Railway in 1863, the Peak was now only three hours from London – a time which even the modern traveller using Inter-City expresses would find hard to beat. Those earliest railway tourists gave fanciful names to the rock formations in Dovedale: Lovers Leap, Reynard's Hall, the Twelve Apostles and Dovedale Church are some examples. Derby poet J. Edwards in his 'Tour of Dove', even heard heavenly music in the dale:

> "O hither bring the harp from Judah's psalms,
> With psaltery, sackbut, dulcimer and lute;
> The music tuned of old to golden psalms
> This crag-built church, these rocky aisles
>   will suit:
> They come – the wilderness no more is mute."

One of the reasons the 'wilderness' of Dovedale was no longer silent may have been the hordes of tourists now flooding in to the dale, some taking advantage of the guided donkey trips available from the Stepping Stones.

In James Crostons's 'On Foot through the Peak' (1876) we learn that litter is not just a modern problem.

> "Reynard's Hall is a favourite resort of the numerous pleasure-seekers and picnic parties who visit Dovedale during the summer months; and the broken glass, orange peel, and other fragmentary remains we find scattered about, tell the story of frolic, feast and fun."

Charles Cotton (1630-1687)

By the 1930s concern was being expressed about the unrestricted development of the British countryside, and a campaign was launched to make Dovedale Britain's first National Park. It was even suggested that a local authority might apply to the Ministry of Health to 'sterilise' the land!

It was against this background of public pressure for the conservation of our finest landscapes and the post-war ambitions of the Labour Government, that the Peak National Park came into being on 17th April 1951.

A selection of Press cuttings dating from the mid-Thirties illustrates the popular pressure at the time to make Dovedale Britain's first National Park. Early purchases by the National Trust helped to make Dovedale a favourite choice.

Dovedale Must Be Saved

THE National Trust Appeal for £13,500 to acquire 1,000 acres of "key" land in the Dovedale—Manifold Valley area must closely touch all ramblers in the Northern area.

For whenever the Dovedale national park ideal is achieved —and the success of the present appeal will bring it appreciably within reach — the walking fraternity in this part of the country will have it on their own doorstep.

M.P.s Want it to Become a National Park.

DEBATE IN THE HOUSE.

[FROM OUR PARLIAMENTARY CORRESPONDENT.]

WESTMINSTER, Wednesday.

A PLEA to make Dovedale a national park, was made in the House of Commons last night by Mr. Geoffrey Mander (Lib., Wolverhampton), in a Private Member's motion.

A NATIONAL PARK AUTHORITY?

AS long ago as 1931 the National Parks Standing Committee urged the Government to set up, without further delay, a National Park Authority ; and just about a year they renewed their recommendation to the Ministry Health. Their latest reinforcements come from the ra of the North-western Naturalists, who at a recent meet at Manchester University recommended immediate ac with regard to Dovedale, Snowdonia, and the Lake Distr There are many other reasons besides those which app primarily to naturalists why national parks should be brou into being, and there are many other areas in the cou besides those mentioned where they ought already to ex

DOVEDALE
The NATIONAL PARK

Dovedale National Park Next Year?

From Our Special Correspondent

BUXTON, Wednesday.

BY the end of 1938 the scheme for the first National Park in Britain—embracing the valleys of the Dove and Manifold and the land lying between them—is likely to be nearing completion, so rapid is progress now being made.

The National Trust, which already owns or protects by covenants several thousand acres in the area, announced yesterday that a further 450 acres have been secured.

About 48 acres, with a long frontage on the River Dove, had been purchased out of funds provided by Sir Robert McDougall, and Cold Eaton Farm has been protected by restrictive covenants over 400 acres.

The new acquisition is of great importance in the scheme.

OBJECTION REMOVED

It fills a gap on the Derbyshire bank of the river between the Trust's properties at Biggin Dale and Iron Tors. Properties owned by the National Trust now stretch for five miles on the Derbyshire side of the river and in addition there are various properties on the Staffordshire bank.

The objection normally raised to National Trust properties forming a basis of a national park—that they are small, scattered units—has been removed in Dovedale.

The Cold Eaton farm land protected has a frontage of about a mile on the main Buxton-Ashbourne road, which is now safe from building development or hoardings. It is here that the first slopes of the Dovedale hills begin, making freedom from development important.

"I am optimistic enough to think that 1938 will see not only the biggest progress yet made towards the scheme for a Dovedale national park, but also a very large extent the completion of it, with the help of the Minister of Health," Mr. F. A. Holmes, honorary secretary of the Dovedale committee of the National Trust, told me today.

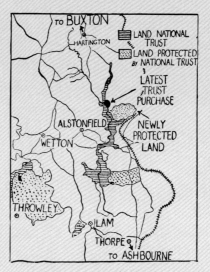

Map showing approximate area of the proposed Dovedale National Park.

OUR FIRST NATIONAL PARK?

THE efforts of the National Trust to obtain possession of a further stretch of beautiful Dovedale and the adjoining Manifold Valley, in the hope that this lovely corner of the Derbyshire and Staffordshire border may become the first of England's National Parks, are such as should be followed with interest by every keen cyclist.

" The Manifold Valley gift will now ensure an eight-miles walk through one of England's most beautiful scenic reserves, and is an important link in the Dovedale National Park scheme.

NATIONAL PARKS.

The movement in favour of the establishment of a number of national parks was stimulated further by the debate in the House of Commons, last night, on a motion for the preservation of areas of natural interest against disorderly development and spoliation, and the improvement of their access to the public.

As was to be expected, Dovedale was one of the areas for which there was a good deal of pleading. Mr. F. A. Holmes, of Buxton, has done a tremendous amount of work with the object of encouraging such a development. Dovedale occupies a central position, within reasonable distance of very large centres of population; its beauty is undisputed, and its historical and literary associations add weight to the demand for its preservation.

FIRST NATIONAL PARK?

General discussion on the question was opened by Alderman Miss F. A. Farmer, of Stoke-on-Trent, who gave evidence before the National Trust Committee. Miss Farmer said that Dovedale would probably be the first National Park in this country. If, however, they merely sat on the fence, all waiting for someone else to make the first move, there was a danger that nothing would be done. Stoke-on-Trent City Council therefore decided to take the initiative and call this Conference, representative of those districts whose inhabitants used Dovedale for the purposes of recreation, education and health.

Mr. Gibbs, expressing the gratitude of the National Trust to Stoke-on-Trent Corporation for calling the Conference, said that the Trust regarded this as a very wise move. He thought that the only way to achieve the preservation of large areas was for all the local authorities and voluntary bodies to co-operate.

The properties accepted by the National Trust—because they were of supreme importance to the Midlands and the nation as a whole—were costly to keep up. It was a general principle of the Trust Committee not to accept any properties as gifts unless some income for maintenance was also provided with them

DOVEDALE PARK ENLARGEMENT

AGAIN Sir Robert McDougall has earned the thanks of the public.

His gift of 48 acres under the Dovedale National Park scheme and his generosity in enabling an additional 400 acres to be safeguarded bring nearer the realisation of the scheme which has been commended in this column from time to time. So near, in fact, that in some quarters it is thought the scheme will be nearing completion by the end of 1938.

Perhaps that is a little optimistic, for much remains to be done. But there can be no doubt that, as Mr. F. A. Holmes, of the Dovedale Committee of the National Trust, says, Sir Robert's gift will give a magnificent impetus to efforts next year.

Dovedale from Thorpe Cloud at the turn of the century.

Dovedale today, showing footpath restoration work, necessary because of extreme visitor pressure.

Today, 40 years on and with over two million visits to Dovedale alone every year, it is sometimes difficult to experience what James Croston described as:

"*A solitude where nought of life is seen,*
A silence that forbids all earthly sound;"

… especially on a summer weekend or Bank Holiday!

And if you asked Byron's question 'Was you ever in Dovedale?' of most visitors today, the answer would probably be 'Yes'.

Today's visitors to the dale come from all walks of life.

The only 'traffic' in this early postcard of
Speedwell Cavern near Castleton, was the
farmer driving his flock of sheep.

Today's traffic is noisier and much more obtrusive, but little else has changed.

Entrance, Speedwell Mine, Castleton

Dovedale was not the only part of the Peak which was popular with early visitors. In fact, probably the earliest tourist guide book to the Peak, 'De Mirabilus Pecci : Concerning the Wonders of the Peak in Darby-shire,' failed to even mention it. This long-winded Latin tour of seven of the Peak's 'Wonders' was written by the philosopher Thomas Hobbes and published in 1636.

The tutor to the Cavendish children at Chatsworth extolled the marvels of Peak Cavern, Eldon Hole, Barmoor Clough's Ebbing and Flowing Well, Mam Tor, Poole's Cavern and St. Ann's Well at Buxton, and Chatsworth itself. Hobbe's list was republished 45 years later by Charles Cotton as 'The Wonders of the Peake' and the seven wonders became an established itinerary for early travellers, such as Daniel Defoe and Celia Fiennes.

Three of the 'wonders' are within walking distance of the village of Castleton, which has been on the tourist trail for centuries. Among the celebrated early visitors were Queen Victoria and Lord Byron. J. B. Firth, in his 'Highways and Byways in Derbyshire', published in 1905, proves that tourist pressure is no new phenomenon:

"Castleton should be given a wide berth on a Saturday or Sunday in the summer months. On these days it overflows with the tripper, for whom it lays itself out to provide, and its streets are apt to be uproarious until the last brakes have gone singing down the vale."

The Industrial Revolution transformed the cities of the Southern Pennines, as places like Manchester and Sheffield became the workshops of the world. The workers who founded the wealth of the British Empire were housed in grim, two-up, two-down terraces, and the only escape from their humdrum existence was the promise of the

Above: Speedwell Cavern was originally a lead mine, and visitors, like these in an Edwardian postcard, are still transported by boat along a flooded canal.

Right: Early guides to Bagshawe Cavern, Bradwell.

weekend's walking on the open, inviting moors of the Peak Ewan MacColl's 'Manchester Rambler' lived for the fact that:

"I may be a wage-slave on Monday,
But I am a free man on Sunday."

Easier communications opened-up the whole of the Peak District, and by the 1930s, walking and climbing in the Peak had become something of a religion to the people in the surrounding cities. Patrick Monkhouse, a 'Manchester Guardian' journalist and later a member of the National Park authority, described the weekend exodus to the Peak in his 'On Foot in the Peak' (1932):

"The movement which has brought young townsfolk out on to the moors has hardly a parallel elsewhere in Britain. For an hour on Sunday mornings it looks like Bank Holiday in the Manchester stations, except that families do not go to Blackpool for Whit-week in shorts. South-countrymen gasp to look at it."

That same year, the pressure for greater access to those Peak moors reached a head with the celebrated Mass Trespass on Kinder Scout, which was led by an 18-year-old unemployed garage mechanic, Benny Rothman. He described, in a BBC 2 documentary, the frustrations felt by those Manchester ramblers:

"Can you imagine the young people walking on the only two footpaths that skirted Kinder Scout, and looking at the rugged rocks on the skyline; seeing the Downfall with its plume of water; and hearing all the stories of what there was on Kinder itself – the peat hags etc? With all that as an incentive, people wanted to go and see these things for themselves. And why not?

The landowners' reason was that the moors of Kinder and Bleaklow were strictly preserved for the raising and shooting of grouse, and Monkhouse describes the tense situation which existed on the route between South Head and Edale Cross:

"There is a faint path, but no right of way, and on a populous Sunday a gamekeeper may be seen sitting with a dog and a gun on the side of South Head. His presence is usually an adequate deterrent, and the gun has not yet been used."

The Thirties saw a booming of interest in rambling and the Great Outdoors.

Climbing and rambling clubs had sprung up in many of the large cities surrounding the Peak. One of the most notable was the Kyndwr Club, founded in 1900 by Sheffield and Derby climbers. But they faced huge problems in gaining access to the moors and crags of the Peak, most of which were strictly private grouse moors, patrolled by burly gamekeepers.

An excerpt from 'High Peak' by Eric Byne and Geoffrey Sutton, describes the situation: "Despite its reputation for ferocious gamekeepers, Kinder Scout also began to receive their attention. Sneaking unnoticed up the Grindsbrook Clough from Edale, they bivouacked under a boulder and the following morning explored the dark, jumbled crags of Nether and Upper Tors, which line the rim of the clough. They found several routes, notably the Primitive and the Promontory, before they were pounced on by angry keepers and hustled down to Edale."

1

3

22

2

4

Burnage Lane
Didsbury
Mch 21/04

Many thanks for
letters & cuttings sent.
Will return cuttings
on Wednesday — I want
to show them to my friend
Jackson. — We had a grand
walk over Kinder

Mr J. W. Puttrell
94 Sheffield Moor
Sheffield

*These pictures show the progress of a trespass
on Kinder in 1904 through a series of
photographic postcards sent to members.
Clockwise from top left: 1. Setting out on the
bridleway from Hayfield to Castleton.
2. In Kinder Clough. 3. A visit to the frozen
Kinder Downfall. 4. In Grindsbrook Clough,
Upper Tor in the background.*

Later, clubs like the Sheffield Clarion Ramblers organised huge open-air rallies in the campaign for access to mountains. This was in The Winnats in 1927.

ALL KINDER PLATEAU OPEN TO WALKERS

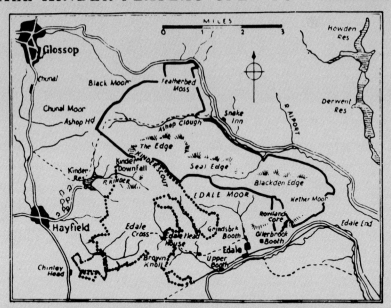

From our Local Government Correspondent

BAKEWELL, TUESDAY.

Access agreements have been concluded between the Peak Park Planning Board and Messrs James Watts, Senior and Junior, covering another 3,354 acres of moorland in the Kinder Scout area. Ramblers now have a legal right to wander over the whole of the Kinder plateau.

This was announced at a meeting of the board here to-day by the chairman of its finance and general purposes committee, Councillor J. E. Roberts. The areas to which the new agreements relate adjoin the 6,000 acres of land belonging to the Chatsworth Settlement and the Youth Hostels Trust which is already subject to access agreements. They include such well-known landmarks as Jacob's Ladder, Edale Cross, Kinder Downfall, the Mermaid's Pool, the Woolpack, and Pym Chair.

Welcoming the announcement, Mr P. Daley expressed the hope that the board would now press on with positive action to open up the rest of the hundred square miles of potential access land in the national park. Councillor Roberts replied that the board had had to spend a great deal of time and trouble in ascertaining who the owners were, and had been negotiating with some of them before it was able to tell them the nature of the by-laws (approved at to-day's meeting) that would protect their properties. He hoped that other landowners would now be more forthcoming and that the agreements already signed would strengthen the board's hands for the use, if necessary, of other powers.

In a comment on the length of time consumed in securing footpath agreements on the Pennine Way, the chairman of the board, Alderman C. F. White, said that too much influence had been brought to bear in London by Manchester's members of Parliament; some of the Derbyshire members also, he added, had not been too helpful.

The board approved a scheme to improve the appearance of derelict tips at the Ecton copper mines, in the Manifold Valley, by the planting of trees in soil pockets on the terraces of the old workings and on the hillside above them. The scheme is to be drawn up by Miss Brenda Colvin, the landscape architect, and will cost about £1,000. Among other projects covered by the estimate—approved to-day—of £38,990 (less £11,950 Government grant) for the board's expenditure in 1955-6 are the provision of a car park at Monsal Head (£5,000) and the purchase of a site for a hostel in Longdendale (£500). Compensation payable under tree preservation orders may amount to £5,000.

The first access agreement, to Kinder, was signed in February, 1955.

Veteran rambler and campaigning outdoor journalist Tom Stephenson had a hidden agenda in proposing, as he did in a Daily Herald feature in 1935, "a Pennine Way from the Peak to the Cheviots." He wanted to crack the long-standing problem of access to the open moors of the Pennines, but could have had no idea how popular his idea would become.

When the Peak National Park came into existence in 1951, one of the first tasks it had to do was to solve the long-standing access problems on the northern moors. The first-ever access agreement with a landowner was signed in 1952, covering 5,780 acres of the northern part of Kinder Scout and the area of Broadlee Bank Tor. Today, some 76 square miles of the National Park are covered by such agreements.

Grindsbrook Clough from Ringing Roger in 1946.

Fifty years after the Pennine Way was first proposed, the Countryside Commission had to sponsor a three-year project in order to look into the severe problems of human erosion affecting this popular 250-mile 'National Trail,' which by this time was being attempted by up to 8,000 people every year, Stephenson's "faint line...engraved on the face of the land" was now a six-lane motorway through Grindsbrook Meadows, and urgent measures were necessary to repair it.

"This need be no Euclidean line...
but just a faint line on the Ordanance Maps"

The same view today, showing the scar of the Pennine Way.

The Peak has been a Mecca for rock-climbers since the days of J. W. Puttrell a Sheffield silversmith who was one of the earliest exponents of the sport in Britain. Puttrell led climbs on Kinder Downfall (above) and did some strenuous back-and-foot work on Wharncliffe Crag (top inset), while other climbers, rather dangerously, climbed three-at-a-time in The Winnats (centre). Modern climbers (bottom inset) take no such risks!

As a playground for people from the surrounding cities, the Peak has been popular since the days of the Kyndwr Club, pictured in a snowbound hut in Grindsbrook in 1906 (right) and descending Eldon Hole in 1904 (bottom left). Some prefer noisy sports, like the motor cycle trial on Stanage Edge in 1961 (top left), or getting away from it all by paragliding (inset) or cycling (far right).

SHELDON 1½ M. TADDINGTON 4 M.
FLAGG 4 M. BUXTON 10 M.
MONYASH 4 M. MANCHESTER 34 M.

Above: Members of a cyclists' touring club relax by the shelter at Ashford-in-the-Water in the early years of the century. (Inset) Modern mountain-bikers are a different breed!

The pressure of the sheer number of visitors, now up to 20 million per annum, was becoming one of the most pressing problems facing the National Park authority. But one of the problems, and the pleasures, of the Peak has always been its accessibility.

The earliest visitors came by horse-drawn coach, charabanc, bicycle or even the new horseless carriage.

"The valley is gone and the Gods with it"

A Buxton-bound goods train crosses the Monsal Dale viaduct around 1912.

"The valley is gone, and the Gods with it; and now, every fool in Buxton can be at Bakewell in half-an-hour, and every fool in Bakewell at Buxton."

Ruskin's celebrated outburst at the completion of the Midland Railway line through Monsal Dale and the Peak District shows the concern felt by this early conservationist at the impact of the railway on the landscape. The line had been completed in 1863, as the Midland Railway Company engaged in cut-throat competition with others to open a line between London and Manchester, passing through what the company grandly called 'Little Switzerland.'

But not everyone shared Ruskin's views, and Edward Bradbury, writing in 'All About Derbyshire' (1884) describes a journey he undertook on the footplate of a Midland express steaming through the Peak.

> *"The windows of the 'bogie' carriage, or the Pullman car, form an ever-changing panorama; but the scenery regarded from the footplate of the speeding engine is a railway romance...my only regret is that I had not John Ruskin for company, to have shown him sentiment in steam, romance in realism, fancy in fact, poetry in points and crossings, sermons in sleepers, songs in steel rails, books in signal-boxes, tongues in trenails, and good in all railway things."*

Time and Nature are great healers, and the magnificent five-arch viaduct at Monsal Dale is now a protected structure, and forms what most people see as a harmonious focus for the ever-popular view from Monsal Head.

The tiny hamlet of Miller's Dale, further up the deep valley of the Wye, had a station which far exceeded the apparent importance of this isolated rural settlement. Two viaducts and no less than five platforms made Miller's Dale a major junction on the Midland line, and it was not uncommon to see five trains at a time occupying the station. The station also had a restaurant and its own Post Office – further indications of just how busy it was.

The Monsal viaduct today, an essential, and protected, part of the scene.

Was Ruskin right? How the scene might look today – without the viaduct.

Miller's Dale Station in its hey-day. The Manchester to St. Pancras express pulls out in August, 1952.

The same scene today, with the north-bound viaduct now a footpath known as the Monsal Trail.

THOR'S CAVE & STATION.

Above: A busy day on the Midland Line at Miller's Dale.

Right: The primrose-yellow coaches of a Manifold Light Railway train draw up at Thor's Cave Station beneath the famous landmark.

The reason for this strange phenomenon was that Miller's Dale was the link between the Midland Line and Buxton, and the branch line from the rapidly-expanding health spa and tourist town joined the main line here. Bradbury describes the scene:

"......a little crowd of passengers awaits the train. Here Mr. Salford, from Manchester, who has left his rheumatism and crutches behind at Buxton, gets nimbly in the express along with Mrs. Salford, and the two Miss Salfords, one a charming symphony in silk, the other a dainty vignette in velvet. Mr. Saltley of Birmingham, very gouty and bound for Buxton, gets out, and there is an interchange of several other passengers. Now the guard blows the whistle to proceed again, and the engine answers with a scream."

Other railways crossed the difficult country of the Peak, the earliest being the Cromford and the High Peak line, originally planned as a canal (its stations were called wharfs) to link the Cromford Canal and the Peak Forest Canal at Whaley Bridge. Opened in 1830 at the very dawn of the Railway Age, the motive power on the level sections was originally by horses, while on the inclines, a clever, continuous cable system was used. The line closed in 1967, and was later to become the High Peak Trail.

Its sister was the unsuccessful Ashbourne-Buxton line, which opened in 1899 but also closed under the Beeching axe in 1967, to eventually be converted by the National Park authority to the Tissington Trail. The Manifold Light Railway, which threaded through the spectacular scenery of the Manifold Valley, was purchased by Staffordshire County Council after closure and became the popular Manifold Track. The last conversion was the Midland line, which is now renamed the Monsal Trail, and there are long-term plans to return steam trains to the route.

Most of the visitors from the surrounding industrial towns and cities came to the Peak by public transport, in the early years of the 20th century. They came by train or charabanc, and there were many regular services from the cities to bring them out into the moors and dales of the Peak. Others came under their own steam, either walking or by bicycle.

But it was the tremendous explosion in car ownership in the latter half of the century which was to have the most dramatic effect on transportation in the Peak.

Top: Tissington Station as it was when the Buxton-Ashbourne line was in operation, contrasts strongly with the view of the same site today (bottom), as a car park and toilet block on the Tissington Trail, a route now used by walkers, cyclists and horse riders.

James Croston described Stoney Middleton in
1876 as "wearing an air of bustling
importance."

One wonders what he would think of the traffic-choked village today?

In the last 30 years, car ownership has doubled in Britain, and the traffic flows on the main roads into the Park have also doubled in the same period. Visitor surveys show that 95 per cent of the Park's 20 million visits are now made by car, and only one per cent by bus.

Increased traffic also brings what Brian Redhead has called 'the paraphernalia of suburbia,' such as unsightly petrol stations, road signs, and of course, bigger and bigger car parks.

The scene in Edale village soon after the Board's ski-tow was opened in 1960.

The village square at Hartington was designed for use as the site of the local fair and market.

Today, like many similar open spaces in villages, it has become a car park.

Calver Sough, a quiet backwater at the turn of the century.

Calver Sough today — signs of the times?

Many roads have had to be widened, or 'improved,' to cope with this increase in traffic. The Winnats Pass road near Castleton had to be upgraded after catastrophic landslips had closed the road below the 'Shivering Mountain' of Mam Tor.

The growth of traffic through the Park is not confined to cars either. Small village communities such as Baslow and Stoney Middleton have been disrupted by the growth of heavy, cross-Park lorry traffic, some emanating from quarries outside the Park itself.

Left: Edwardian cyclists dismount to descend The Winnats Pass, near Castleton.

Above: The Winnats now carries the main Castleton to Chapel-en-le-Frith road.

Surveyors Fear Rock Avalanche Here

Corner of the **Mam Tor** road, showing the loose and rocky nature of the mountainside.

The surveyors were right! The Mam Tor road finally collapsed and was abandoned in 1977, diverting traffic through The Winnats.

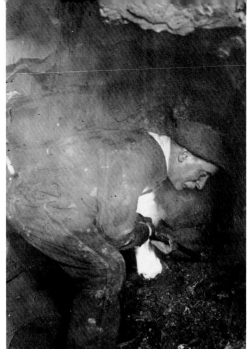

Although most modern visitors are attracted to the Peak for its apparently unspoilt scenery and the absence of industrial development, the fact is that industry of one kind or another has played an important role in shaping the landscape.

For centuries the livelihood of many Peaklanders was founded on the dual economies of farming and mining, and most farmers in the White Peak area also had a share in the lead mines which dotted the limestone plateau.

Left: Transferring the title of a lead mine at Greaves Croft, Moss Rake, Bradwell, 1906.

Above: Drilling out a new level in the Cupola Lead Mine, Middleton Dale.

Lead mining has a long and complex history in this part of the Peak. The first to exploit these underground riches were the Romans, and the fort of Navio, near Brough, is thought to have been built to protect these mineral interests.

Above left: A hand-operated jigging machine, used to separate lead ore from waste gangue, at a Bradwell lead mine. Above right: Modern limestone quarrying requires more sophisticated machinery.

Right: A horse-drawn crushing circle, used to crush lead ore.

The Hope Valley from Bradwell Edge at the
turn of the century shows an open, treeless
landscape, but many small lead mines existed
underground.

Today's view from the same place is dominated by the cement works chimney and associated quarries, and the growing village of Bradwell in the foreground.

A classic historic landscape illustrating the dual economy of the White Peak, near the Miners' Standard, Winster. These field barns were used both for farming and lead mining. The top photograph was taken in 1970, but the bottom one, taken more recently, shows the sad state of the barns today.

But the real hey-day of the lead mining industry was in the mid 18th century, when at least 10,000 miners were at work in the White Peak area governed by a complex set of laws administered by ancient Barmote Courts. A successful mine, in the 1730s, extracted lead worth £50,000 in three years – a fortune in those days.

Lead wasn't the only mineral plundered from the Peak landscape, either. The Ecton Copper Mines, in the valley of the Manifold in Staffordshire, were among the richest in the country, and were estimated to have earned the Duke of Devonshire a profit of £1.3 million during the 18th century. They were worked for three centuries and made a significant impact on the landscape. Less obtrusive were the mines from which the semi-precious Blue John stone was taken in the Treak Cliff area near Castleton, and the decorative Ashford 'Black Marble' (a polished limestone) mines at Asford-in-the-Water.

Most villages also had their own local quarry for building stone, but limestone and gritstone quarries in those days were small by comparison with today's massive developments with their associated machinery. But even in the days of the earliest tourists, some people were upset by the impact of industry. James Croston, in 'On

Foot through the Peak' (1876) complained about a lead smelting cupola chimney, near the site of the present Hope Valley Cement Works;

"*About a mile from Castleton, close to the road side, a cupola smelting furnace has been erected, the huge circular black chimney of which forms a conspicuous object, and may be seen from almost every part of the dale.*"

The Hope Valley Cement Works, which was in operation long before the National Park came into existence, illustrates the quarrying quandary faced by the National Park authority. An important local source of employment (over 300 local people work there), it is an economic fact of life in the Hope Valley, and produces about 1.3 million tonnes of cement a year – about 10 per cent of the UK total.

But the increased demand for raw materials and the accessibility of Peak District reserves has seen the quarrying industry make bigger and bigger demands on the National Park landscape. In 1989, 7.4 million tonnes of limestone was extracted from the ten major Peak District quarries, most of it destined for road aggregate.

The Peak District's reserves of fluorspar, formerly an unwanted by-product of lead

mining, are the most important in the country. Laporte's Cavendish Mill, near Stoney Middleton, now produces about 80,000 tonnes of fluorspar a year – about 70 per cent of the total UK supply.

In the old days, the main use of Peak limestone was local, either for building stone or, after burning in lime kilns, for application on the land to 'sweeten' acidic pastureland. Many farms had their own lime kilns, while others sprang up alongside railway lines, like the Midland line, where the treated lime was sent direct for industrial as well as agricultural use.

Of all the industries which have taken place in the Peak, the oldest, and the one which has made the most significant impact, is undoubted farming. Farming has shaped the face of the Peak over the past 10,000 years, starting from the initial clearance of the native woodland by the first Stone Age settlers.

Top: Burned lime being applied to fields below the Roaches.

Bottom: Sheep washing has turned into a tourist attraction at Ashford in the Water today, but previously (inset) it was an everyday farming task.

The main picture shows the neat pattern of drystone walls, many of which follow the lines of medieval strip fields, to the east of Castleton, as they looked at the turn of the century. The modern picture (inset) shows the same scene today, with many walls gone as they have become redundant to the farmers' needs.

But the single most impressive legacy which generations of Peak District farmers have left is surely the network of drystone walls, which covers so much of the National Park landscape. Most of these walls date from the Enclosure Acts of the 18th and 19th centuries, although some have recently been proved to be of Roman foundation. They have impressed generations of visitors since the intrepid Celia Fiennes, who travelled alone on side-saddle through the Peak in 1697 and noted: "...you see neither hedge nor tree but only low drye stone walls round some ground, else its only hills and dales as thick as you can imagine...."

In the White Peak (limestone) area alone, it has been estimated that there are 26,000 miles of drystone walls, and they form a lasting impression to visitors, especially those, like Celia Fiennes, who come from the south. The National Park authority has recognised the importance of these walls in the landscape, and through its Farm Conservation Scheme, has grant-aided farmers to rebuild over 30 miles and to maintain a further 90 miles.

The problem is that, in the modern depressed agricultural climate, many Peak District farms are regarded as marginal, (or 'less favoured' in Eurospeak) and wall repair and maintenance has not been high on the farmers' list of priorities. But, as we have seen in this book, landscapes are constantly changing and who knows what the next century will bring?

Drystone walling is an ancient craft which is being encouraged by the National Park authority through farm management grants.

Right: Cressbrook Mill in its hey-day looked like an imposing Georgian mansion. Today (above) it is a crumbling building in search of a new role.

One of the biggest problems faced by Peak lead miners was water, which flooded and made inaccessible many potentially productive lead veins. Special drainage tunnels, known as soughs (pronounced 'suffs', were constructed to 'unwater' many mines, but paradoxically, it was the power of that water which was to be the foundation of another important Peakland industry.

Some of the imposing cotton mills which sprang up in the Peak District dales during the 18th century were actually powered by the waters from these lead mine soughs, and for a time, the area became the cradle of the emergent Industrial Revolution. Richard Arkwright's 1771 Cromford Mill, just outside the Park, was the first to use water power, in this case the mighty River Derwent. Within the next decade, Arkwright had built further mills at Cromford, and at Cressbrook and Bakewell in the valley of the River Wye.

The present Cressbrook Mill, an imposing, pedimented building like a Georgian mansion nestling in the Wye valley, is not Arkwright's. His original mill was burnt down in 1785, and the present building dates from 1814. It and its sister mill at Litton about a mile upstream, present the National Park authority with many problems now that they are no longer needed for their original use. Various

proposals have been made for new uses for these listed and protected buildings, but they have to be compatible with National Park objectives and acceptable to local residents.

As the industrial cities which surround the Peak expanded in the wake of the Industrial Revolution, water also became an important commodity for their rapidly-increasing populations. An unpolluted atmosphere, high rainfall and deep, thinly-populated valleys made the Peak District an ideal place to site the reservoirs which were to feed the thirsts of the new industrial cities.

Litton Mill, about a mile upstream in the valley of the Wye, spawned a hamlet of workers' cottages. It became notorious for the ill-treatment of its young apprentices.

The Vale of Ashopton before the construction of the Ladybower Reservoir.

Opposite page: The same scene today. The white arches of Ashopton viaduct standing over the site of Ashopton village.

*Derwent village (above) and Ashopton village
(right) were both submerged under the
reservoir in the 1940's.*

Derwent village in the trees.

A corner of Derwent village.

Huge expanses of water now fill about 50 Dark Peak dales, where thriving farming communities once existed. The coming of the reservoirs from the late 19th century transformed many valleys into an entirely unnatural, though not unlovely landscape.

The classic site is the Upper Derwent Valley, which was flooded by a series of dams and reservoirs starting from the Howden and Derwent Dams, which were constructed between 1901 and 1916. They were followed, between 1935 and 1943, by the Ladybower Reservoir, to form the most extensive area of man-made water space in the Peak, and an area now very popular with visitors.

While the Derwent and Howden dams in the upper reaches of the valley merely flooded isolated farmhouses, the two ancient hamlets of Derwent, with its Jacobean hall, and Ashopton were submerged beneath the rising waters of the Ladybower reservoir. According to Ray Ollerenshaw, a local farmer, the local communities were quite active:

> *"We used to have a whist drive and dance every fortnight at Derwent School, even through the winter, and you could see the lamps of people coming across the mountains, down from the outlying farms at Two Thornfields and Lockerbrook. Everybody came."*

When the reservoir was proposed, there was much local opposition, because they could see it was the end of their traditional way of life. But it didn't make any difference:

> *"The locals were very annoyed about the planned reservoir and got up a petition, but there weren't enough of us to make a shout. Anyway, before the locals knew anything about it, the landowners had already sold up to the Water Board."*

After the building of the reservoir, the people of Derwent and Ashopton were rehoused in purpose-built houses at Yorkshire Bridge, below the huge embankment of the Ladybower Dam. The ancient Derwent packhorse bridge which had been in the centre of the village, was dismantled and stored, eventually to be reconstructed in memory of the Sheffield rambler, John Derry, at Slippery Stones at the head of the valley.

While two communities were destroyed by the construction of the Ladybower Reservoir, another had been created by the construction of the Derwent and Howden dams. Birchinlee village, popularly known as 'Tin Town' because most of its buildings were made of corrugated iron, housed a population of over 1,000 navvies and their families while the earlier dams were under construction. This self-contained community was complete with shops, a recreation hall, hospital, canteen and police station. The site is now forgotten and hidden under the ranks of conifers which cloak the side of the valley.

Even earlier than the Derwent dams were those which were constructed in Longdendale, in the far north of the Park. Here, the string of five reservoirs which flooded the valley of the Etherow between 1848 and 1875 were, in their time, the largest expanse of man-made water in the world.

Top: Derwent Hall, a former shooting lodge owned by the Duke of Norfolk and later one of the first youth hostels in the Peak, viewed from across the ancient packhorse bridge. Right: The reconstructed packhorse bridge at Slippery Stones, above the reservoirs. It was re-erected in 1959 in memory of John Derry, a Sheffield journalist and guidebook author.

The navvies' village of 'Tin Town' at Birchinlee, as seen from across the River Derwent at Abbey Bank in 1904. (Inset) The upper road of Birchinlee village.

The same scene today, with all trace of Tin Town gone, replaced by the blocks of conifers planted by the water company to aid water purification.

Over on the western side of the Park, the scenic Goyt valley was similarly used by the water engineers to supply water to Stockport by the construction of the Fernilee and Errwood Reservoirs.

But as the appreciation of the landscape heightened and the National Park authority came into existence, other reservoir proposals were opposed and successfully stopped. These included proposals for Hassop, near Bakewell, and Brund, near Longnor in the Upper Manifold Valley.

There was strong local opposition to this last proposal, led by the Manifold Valley Preservation Committee and supported by the National Park authority. In the foreword to a booklet 'The Manifold – a fight for life' published in 1971, Sir John Betjeman wrote:

"I am one of the thousands who enjoy this superb part of the Peak Park and every effort must be made to resist the proposed reservoir on this site.

Top: The remains of Goytsclough Mill, used latterly for making paint, in the village of Goyts Bridge. Bottom: The Goyt Valley, before the reservoirs. Inset: Sailing on the Errwood Reservoir.

"The Manifold Valley is a pedestrian's paradise. It is of national importance in our fast disappearing stretches of country landscape. The fact that it is part of a National Park is a proof of how highly it is regarded. In some places a Reservoir can improve the landscape, but not in this one."

The plan was abandoned, and the reservoir eventually approved at Carsington, outside the National Park.

Top: Errwood Hall, Italianate home of the Grimshawe family, was built in 1830 and surrounded by beautiful gardens. It was demolished in the mid-1960s when the Errwood Reservoir was built, and is now a picturesque ruin (right), surrounded by pinewoods, rhododendron and azalea bushes, and very popular with visitors.

The most striking change in our 'before and after' photographs of the dales is the amazing increase in the amount of tree cover.

There are several reasons for this, the most important being the decrease in the amount of grazing which happened for a number of complex reasons. As improvements in farming took place, the heathlands of the limestone plateau were swiftly converted to productive pasture, and the quality of the stock was also improved by selective breeding. Farmers were reluctant to risk these more valuable beasts on the sparse and rocky slopes of the dales.

Dairying also became more important in the 19th century, and stock was taken from the relatively poor pastures of the dale sides to the improved ones on the plateau. From here, their milk could be more easily transported via the new railway lines to the neighbouring fast-growing towns and cities. All these factors combined to lessen grazing pressure on the dales, and without the nibbling teeth of sheep and cattle to keep them under control, trees were able to establish themselves and flourish.

Indeed, several authorities have forecast that without careful management, the dales could soon revert to woodland through natural succession.

More recently, the ever-increasing number of visitors and their dogs has made modern farmers much less willing to graze their sheep in the dales. Visiting the dales was a trend started by those early guidebooks, but even they could not have envisaged the numbers of today.

John Ruskin (1819-1901) wrote:

"The whole gift of the country is in its glens. The wide acreage of field or moor above is wholly without interest; it is only in the clefts of it, and the dingles, that the traveller finds his joy."

Early tourists like Ruskin were attracted to the Peak District by the amazing natural rock architecture of the dales. It was they who gave fanciful names to the rock formations in places like Dovedale, and marvelled at the 'sublime' grandeur of the scenery.

In 'Black's Picturesque Guide to Alton Towers and Dovedale' (1870) Llewellywn Jewitt describes Dovedale thus: "For its picturesque beauties, its wild passes, its gorgeous woods, its magnificent rocks, its beautiful river, and the wonderous variety of its scenery, it is unrivalled by any other in the kingdom."

Left: Sough Mill, in lower Lathkill Dale.

Above: Tree growth has made the same scene virtually unrecognisable today.

Ilam Rock, Dovedale, at the turn of the century.

It's hard to believe but this was taken from the same spot today.

Middleton Dale, looking west, at the turn of the century, showed towering limestone cliffs and ivied buttresses. (Inset top) Today's view from the same spot is entirely choked by trees – and fast-moving traffic on the A623. (Inset bottom) F.L. Chantrey's engraving in 'Peak Scenery' (1818) romantically exaggerated the buttress of Castle Rock in Middleton Dale.

James Croston, in his 'On Foot Through the Peak' (1876), refers to the journey from Eyam to Stoney Middleton along Middleton Dale "...the scenery...is eminently picturesque, and for wildness and stern grandeur is hardly equalled in the Peak...On the left hand side of the dale rugged and weather-beaten crags, abrupt and vast, rise to a height of 300 or 400 feet, their cold grey colour agreeably harmonising with the mosses and lichens that chequer their channelled sides".

But photographs of the dales comparing these turn of the century scenes with those of today show enormous changes, and not just in the increase in tree cover. Dales which have roads running through them, like Middleton Dale and Bradwell Dale, now suffer from an almost constant rush of traffic, making it difficult for the modern visitor to appreciate their beauties anyway.

So the rock features which first fascinated the early tourists and which can be seen in early photographs and postcards are today often obscured by trees and traffic.

Top: The Hathersage to Grindleford road, near Leam Woods looking north towards Stanage Edge, from an early postcard. Bottom: The plantations of Leam Woods obscure the road completely in this modern view.

A photograph of Bakewell about the turn of the century, taken from a glass plate negative, shows a settlement clustered around the crossing of the Wye, the church, and the market.

A modern photograph from the same viewpoint shows the expansion of the town, with housing estates spreading especially up the hill to the west of the town centre.

TIDESWELL NEW BANK BUILDINGS, 1909

Most Peak District villages were in existence by the time of the Domesday Survey in 1086. But in an upland area like this, settlements were small and scattered and based on the traditional industries of mining and farming. Sometimes, villages were created at important crossroads or near fords across rivers, and sometimes they grew around a focal point like the village pond, or mere.

The exceptions were those larger villages which served as market places for the surrounding farmsteads. Most of these ancient markets emerged through a succession of royal charters granted between 1200 and 1350, the earliest in the Peak being at Hartington in 1203. King John granted William de Ferrers the right to hold a Wednesday market and a three-day fair on the festival of St. Giles.

Castleton won its right to hold a market in 1222, while Tideswell followed in 1251 and Bakewell in 1254. Of these larger villages, only Bakewell seems to have existed as a large centre before the Norman Conquest. It is first mentioned in the Anglo-Saxon Chronicle as a fortress of Edward the Elder, so today's weekly Monday market could be as much as 1,000 years old.

A sequence of photographs from Tideswell which records the development of the site of the Old Guild Hall of St. Mary. The first photograph shows the Guild Hall in a ruinous state in 1904; the second, its demolition in 1909, and the last its replacement by a new bank building opened shortly afterwards.

Bear-baiting was a popular 'sport' at medieval fairs, but by the time this photograph was taken at Tideswell Wakes Fair around the turn of the century, the bear was merely an exotic sideshow.

These ancient markets existed not only for the buying and selling of farm livestock. Other goods and chattels were bought and sold, and the market served an important social function of bringing together folk from a wide rural area.

There were also annual fairs, usually on the feast day of the patron saint of the parish church, when other attractions were brought in for the entertainment of the people. These events are echoed in today's Wakes Week activities, which survive in many villages, often now associated with well-dressings or customs like Castleton's ancient Garlanding Ceremony.

Many of the larger villages had important churches, like Bakewell and Tideswell, and in medieval times they saw the foundation of guilds often again associated with the patron saint of the church. The medieval guilds, like that of St. Mary at Tideswell (which was founded around 1349) were voluntary organisations not unlike the more modern friendly societies. A 1922 guidebook to Tideswell mentions the Old Guild Hall "which for so long stood in a ruinous condition in the centre of the town, not far from the parish church".

Top: A rare photograph of one of the last shepherds' gatherings at the now-demolished Miller's Arms, Saltersbrook, at the head of the Woodhead Pass.

Bottom: Farmers and stallholders gather for the Hartington Beef Fair outside the former Volunteers' Arms (now a village shop) in Hartington Market Place.

Top: Well-dressing, once a purely community affair as the picture of Longnor shows, has now become a major tourist attraction, as in the inset photograph taken at Youlgrave.

The local 'big-house' was often the scene of the tea party at the conclusion of the village gala. This charming photograph (left), shows an Edwardian gathering of almost the entire village of Cressbrook, including the silver band, at Cressbrook Hall.

Castleton, from the slopes of Castle Hill at the turn of the century, shows a bleak, treeless landscape, with the newly-constructed building of Losehill Hall with its stable block, prominent in the distance.

The same scene today not only shows more trees in the landscape, but also the expansion of the village as a tourist destination, witnessed by the car park (left). Losehill Hall, now the National Park's Study Centre, is now hidden by the trees.

Early conservationists, like the Council for the Protection of Rural England, were concerned in the Thirties at the proliferation of enamel advertising signs like these, outside the village shop in The Square, Castleton.

Today, The Old Barn caters mainly for the tourist trade, and the shop has expanded into the barn from which it takes its name.

So villages developed as the trading centres for large areas of countryside, and shops opened up in their main streets. These would sell everything from groceries to saddlery, and their front window displays became a matter of some pride to the shopkeepers.

As the populations expanded in the 18th and 19th centuries, the village schools became important buildings in the social and cultural life of the community. They are still the indicator of a thriving village, although sadly many of the smaller village schools which have served the community for a century or more have been forced to close because of the falling numbers of pupils. Cottages have also been bought up by 'in-comers' and some are now holiday cottages, empty for half the year.

Proud custodians of the village shop, Bradwell were the Walker family, represented here by Mary Alice Walker and young Wilf, standing at the door.

The entire roll of Brandside School (six pupils) on the day it finally closed in the early seventies.

The traditional Peak District village was a self-sufficient community, with craftsmen and tradespeople to serve every need. Villagers were able to feed themselves from their allotments, which often spread outside the confines of the village itself, and many fattened their own livestock, such as pigs, in their back gardens.

Some village street scenes have hardly changed in nearly 200 years. Francis Chantrey's engraving of the village street and Plague Cottages in Eyam in 1818 (top) is instantly recognisable today (right). The only changes are the drained mere (left) and the village stocks (right), which have been moved onto the green.

The buildings of the village were constructed from local stone – limestone in the White Peak and gritstone in the Dark – and most villages had their own quarry for building stone (which can often still be identified) on their outskirts. Roofing was either by thatch (heather or reed) or the heavy gritstone slates, which were later often replaced by the durable blue Welsh slates from Snowdonia.

Newer developments have to be carefully controlled and regulated by the National Park authority if the character of these villages is not to be destroyed.

Top: The self-sufficiency of villages is illustrated in these two photographs of Youlgrave. The main picture shows Bankside as it was, with rows of neatly-walled gardens and allotments leading down towards Bradford Dale, while the inset shows the same scene today.

Right: An interesting pair of pictures from Monyash showing cottages in Chapel Street before and after restoration. The first picture (left) shows a part-thatched, part-tiled cottage on the right. This was a common practice when stone slates were expensive, and it was felt important to protect the walls from run-off. The thatching was probably of heather.

The problem with good conservation is that it is often invisible. Much of the work which the National Park authority has done over the past 40 years is not obvious to the casual visitor, because the achievement has been in keeping things looking relatively natural. But the pressures on the Peak are, if anything, growing, and the difficult balancing act between conservation, recreation and the local interest becomes harder year by year.

Visitor pressure has emerged as one of the major problems facing the Park, and with numbers now over 20 million per annum, urgent measures will soon be required to prevent it from becoming a victim of its own popularity. The photographs from Dovedale at the start of this book graphically illustrate this point. In one sense, it could be seen as a tribute to the success of the Park authority, for although it never actively promotes the place, it is the unspoilt scenery which is the main attraction for most visitors.

Pressures and changes in the future may be completely outside the National Park authority's control. The demand for minerals, for example, is dictated by the state of the economy, as are major road improvements. Changes in farming policy are also often influenced by the European Community, and as we have seen, it is the farmers who have largely shaped the Peak landscape over the centuries. New support arrangements for farmers could quickly change the appearance of the Peak, just as they have in the past. No one can be sure what the farmed landscape will look like in the future.

Likewise, many of the landscape improvements carried out by the Park, such as tree planting or footpath restoration, will probably look much better in 20 or 30 years time, when they have 'weathered-in' to the landscape.

Among the other positive achievements by the National Park authority have been its Farm Conservation Scheme, which in its first three years generated £850,000-worth of conservation work on Peak farms, from 'pump-priming' grants totalling £380,000. The Board's Historic Buildings Grant Scheme, started in 1976, has provided nearly £1 million-worth of funding in over 800 schemes aimed at saving the National Park's built heritage. Access agreements have been negotiated covering over 76 square miles of those once-forbidden moors in the north of the Park, allowing free access to ramblers for most of the year. In fact, 60 per cent of access land in Britain is in the Peak National Park.

The Park's resident population of 38,000 has been helped in other ways. Light industrial estates have been encouraged at Bakewell, Tideswell, Longnor and Warslow, creating jobs for local people. And low-cost housing schemes for young local people have been approved at Longnor, Great Longstone, Hartington, Tideswell and other villages.

Among the 'invisible' benefits the National Park authority has achieved by successfully opposing harmful developments have been the stopping of a proposed 200 mph Grand Prix motor racing circuit around Monyash and Arbor Low; the threat of a motorway standard road and a CEGB pumped storage scheme in Longdendale; the construction of a huge reservoir near Brund in the Manifold Valley, and, more recently, major extensions to limestone quarries at Topley Pike and Eldon Hill.

As we said at the start of this book, landscapes will always change, and we can never know how or when. Much the same sort of outcry was made at the destruction of the open field system when the Enclosure Movement started in the 18th century as is made now when hedges are grubbed out or drystone walls allowed to deteriorate. John Clare, the Northamptonshire nature poet, bitterly complained:

*"Inclosure, thou'rt a curse upon the land
And tasteless was the wretch who thy existence
plann'd."*

Who is to say the same sort of protest might not greet the possible demolition of the historic Hope Valley Cement Works in years to come?

Man's influence on the landscape of the Peak has generally been harmonious – the pattern of drystone walls blends perfectly with the limestone crags in Dam Dale, near its junction with Peter Dale.

Notes on the Photography

It's click click every trip for the millions of visitors who each year set off in their cars for the Peak District. Who of us goes on holiday or spends a day out in the country today without taking a camera with us? With modern cameras, it is often no more trouble than slipping a small compact into a pocket.

Years ago however, it was very different. With large plate cameras and their weighty accessories, a packhorse rather than a pocket might have been more suitable for some locations in the Peak. Needless to say, photography in its early days was the preserve of professionals and a few hardy amateurs.

Then in 1888, Kodak introduced a camera that was to change all that and eventually make photography available to everyone. It was a small box camera, seven inches long by four inches wide, and for the first time it was capable of taking roll film. It also came ready loaded with enough film to make 100 exposures – and what's more, Kodak did the processing and printing as well.

It was now possible for anyone to take photographs almost anywhere, but at £10 for the camera and film and £4 for processing (a lot of money in those days), photography was mainly the preserve of the more affluent.

So at the turn of the century, camera ownership was still rare but certainly affordable to many of the early tourists who came to the Peak, and they provide the source of many of the old photographs used in this book.

Just like today's tourists, they wanted to show the beautiful places they had visited, and consequently we have inherited a photographic record which shows only the more picturesque places.

Bearing this in mind, it is not surprising that the 'before' and 'after' photographs in this book leave the impression that the Peak District landscape has changed for the worse.

It is unlikely that the modern tourist would have taken photographs of the Peak from the modern viewpoints we have used here, for there are many better viewpoints from which to show the splendours which still exist in the National Park. This is evident in the numerous modern guide books which include photographs of an idyllic countryside, and it would not be unreasonable to speculate that, if comparable old photographs were available from the same viewpoints, we might see a Peak District which had changed for the better. But the fact is there are few old photographs of unattractive places – photographers don't often take that sort of picture!

I have tried to be honest in taking today's photographs from exactly the same viewpoint as the old ones. But by choosing a particular moment it is possible to interpret areas in very different ways. Stoney Middleton on page 41 and Dovedale on page 10 can still be very quiet early on Sunday mornings. While a scene of peace and tranquillity could have been portrayed in both places, I have chosen moments in which to show what I see as problems which relate to these places.

While the last two examples may exaggerate a change, the evidence of increased tree and scrub growth as discussed on pages 65-69 is probably much underestimated. The viewpoint comparable to many of the old photographs is now occupied by dense woodland and, with the exception of one perilous example, those viewpoints have now gone and the evidence of change with them.

They say the camera never lies, but the evidence of some of the 'before and after' photographs in this book may prove that perhaps sometimes, it can be economical with the truth.

Ray Manley

Acknowledgements

Many people too numerous to mention individually have helped in the production of this book by generously lending photographs for copying and by providing information.

We thank particularly: Nat Allen; J.M. Bentley; Mrs. Beresford; Eddie Blackburn; Mrs Boyce; Nic Broomhead; Malcolm Burton; Linda Bussey; Buxton Museum; Ken Campbell; Castleton Historical Society; the late F. Chapman; George Challenger; the late Mrs. Cotterill; Council for the Protection of Rural England (Sheffield and Peak branch); Derbyshire County Museum; the late Mrs. Evans; Brian Jones; L. M. Hobdey; the Institute of Agricultural History; E. R. Morten; Ken Munns; Ray Ollerenshaw; George Oxley; the late W. A. Poucher; Ron Priestley; Muriel Shirt; Severn Trent Water plc; Peter Townsend; Mark Vallance, and Mike Williams.

Back to the future? The great shark's fin of Parkhouse Hill emerges from the mists in the Upper Dove Valley, echoing its birth as reef limestone 330 million years ago, at the genesis of the Peak District.